Sleeping Beauty

A Family Pantomime

Guy Unsworth

Author's Note

A great pantomime feels live, local and up to date. Therefore, a license to perform this comes with full permission for you to tailor it to your own production and audience.

Character List

CARABOSSE
The Wicked Queen. Aunt of Luna. Evil, vicious, acerbic, sharp. Exceptionally high status and enjoys asserting it. Jealous and bitter towards Luna. A master of disguise and transformation.

FAIRY-FIZZ
Aside from her awesome magical powers, Fizzy's just like one of us. Oh and she's super cool, super fun and a happiness super-spreader.

LUNA
Born a Princess but doesn't know it. Grew up with Maris and Spud. Determined, independent, knows her own mind. Fights for the greater good, sometimes without considering the consequences. She's the people's best friend.

DAME MARIS PIPER
Mother to Spud and surrogate mother to Luna. Has worked all her life to keep a roof over her head. She knows the true danger of Carabosse and avoids it at all costs. She is desperate to find love.

SPUD PIPER
Son of Maris. Not the brightest bulb on the tree, but never lacking in enthusiasm. Silly and charming.

PRINCE ISTUNA
Prince of the neighbouring Kingdom of Coggeshall. Charming but inexperienced at dating. Princely, yes, but kind of goofy too.

POLO
A Pet Penguin. Luna's best friend. Funny, cheeky, great at hugs.

TIMOTHY
Prince Istuna's equerry and right hand man

An **ENSEMBLE** of townsfolk, fairies, demons, dragons and penguins

* Casting is encouraged to be flexible and imaginative *

This edition of **SLEEPING BEAUTY** was the rehearsal script for the **MERCURY THEATRE, COLCHESTER** 2023-24 pantomime season. The cast and creative team were as follows:

CAST
Luna - Alexandra Barredo
Male Ensemble - Nick Brittain-Keates
Prince Istuna - Philip Catchpole
Polo - Matthew Forbes
Fairy Fizz - Sasha Latoya
Carabosse - Jaimie Pruden
Female Ensemble - Shelby Speed
Dame Maris Piper - Antony Stuart Hicks
Spud Piper - Dale Superville

MUSICIANS
Musical Director/Keys - Paul Herbert
Electric & Bass Guitar - Harley Johnston
Alto Sax, Tenor Sax & Flute - Stephanie Frankland
Drums & Percussion - David Pack

CREATIVES
Director - Ryan McBryde
Designer - Jasmine Swan
Lighting Designer - Matt Ladkin
Sound Designer - Nico Menghini
Musical Director - Paul Herbert
Choreographer - Rosie Mather
Casting Directors - Jenkins McShane CDG, Lucy Jenkins, Sooki McShane
Assistant Director - Chani Merrell*
*6 month placement through the Birkbeck, University of London Director's Scheme

ENSEMBLE
Albie Keeble
Miguel Benerayan
Chloe Cheung
Xavana Blake
Kacey Speakman
Niamh Butcher
Nathan Smith
Daisie McIntyre
Leo Wiggins
Scarlett Brothers
Annabel Nottage
Misan Idowu
Archie Kropidlowski
Zara Ball
Dexter Inman
Shanta-May Boodoo

PRODUCTION MANAGEMENT
Producer - Tracey Childs
Production Manager - Jeremy Naunton
Assistant Producer - Jenny Moore

WORKSHOP
Head of Construction - Philip Attwater
Deputy Workshop Manager - Harriet Bonner
Workshop Assistant - Jim Bonner
Scenic Carpenter - Rob van der Parker
Scenic Artists - Rhiannan Howell, Simon Sharman, David Thomas,
Louise Worrall

WARDROBE
Costume Supervisor & Costume Maker - Corinna Vincent
Deputy Costume Supervisor & Costume Maker - Chantelle Regan
Wardrobe Supervisor & Headdress Maker - Lucinda Cawdron
Wardrobe Assistants - Cathy Court, Alice Powell

STAGE MANAGEMENT
Company Stage Manager - Rebecca Samuels
Deputy Stage Manager (On the Book) - Emilie Leger
Assistant Stage Manager (Book Cover) - Lucy Quinton
Assistant Stage Managers - Gillian McGrath, Marjanne van der Parker

TECHNICAL
Technical Manager - Emily Holmden Kingsman
Senior Stage Technician - Roger Mills Lewis
Lighting Programmer - Alex Forey
Lighting Operator - Hazuki Mogan
Followspot Operators - Adam Lloyd and Travis Roxburgh
Stage Crew (Lead) - Sam Copus
Stage Crew - Joey Hawken, Sam Swaine
Flyman - Alex Ray
Sound No.1 - Marco Carpegna
Sound No.2 - Wesley Laing
Technical Swings - Lara Carey, Mike Young

MARKETING TEAM
Nathan Garwood
Rhianna Howard
Bea Maynard
Jack Pederson
Molly Richardson

CHAPERONES
Lissy Campbell
Sue Campbell
Diane Emberton
Tamsin Jones
Paul Kusel-Baum
Elaine Lloyd
Sarah Lloyd
Debra Morgan
Heidi Speakman
Ann Taylor
Niki Taylor
Maggie Walton
Jacquie Woodland

Scene List

ACT ONE

Scene 1 - The Forest

SONG: Overture

> *Musical flourish. Flash. FAIRY FIZZ appears. Underscore.*

FAIRY FIZZ
Hello Colchester - guess who this is
I'm packed full of goodness, my name's Fairy Fizz,
With magic and music there's no need to fear
If you're here for some fun, let's hear you cheer.

(Audience cheer.)

F to the I to the Zed Zed why? She's Fizzy!
(Whoop! Whoop!)
She's Fizzy! Oh yeah.

That's right Colchester - this is ya girl Fairy Fizz. I am a self-confessed, self-employed, self-helping Fairy and I have just landed the contract of a lifetime - to look after you lot and the great sun-kissed city of Colchester! Do you wanna be my fizzy friends? **(Yes)** I said do you? **(Yes)**. Fizzzzztastic! In that case, every time I come on...

> *She encourages the audience to join in.*

F to the I to the Zed Zed why? She's Fizzy!
(Whoop! Whoop!)
She's Fizzy! Oh yeah.

> *Beat continues underneath.*

That's wicked everyone. However, pals, not all is hunky dory here in Colchester these days and that's why I'm here to help our wonderful hero called Luna **(cheer)**, so that she can defeat the treacherous villain Queen Carabosse **(boo)**. That's right, to help our hero Luna **(cheer)**, defeat the villain Queen Carabosse **(boo)**. Do you want to hear a story folks? **(Yes)**. Alright Fizz-kids - story mode on. Let's get audio Fizzual.

SONG: BACKSTORY RAP[1]
(FRESH PRINCE OF BEL AIR:)

> NOW THIS IS A TALE OF EVIL AND GOOD
> SO MAKE SURE ALL IS UNDERSTOOD
> NOW I'D LIKE TO TAKE A MINUTE CAUSE IT IS MY DUTY,
> TO INTRODUCE A STORY KNOWN AS SLEEPING BEAUTY

Lights up through the gauze on the KING and QUEEN holding baby wrapped in gold christening dress.

> IN A CASTLE A BABY CAME ON TO THE SCENE
> WHERE HER PARENTS WERE CURRENTLY THE KING AND THE QUEEN
> HER LIFE WAS THE BEST, IT WAS FULL OF AFFECTION
> THE ROYAL FAM'LY? HASHTAG PERFECTION!

> THEN THE QUEEN'S SISTER - UP TO NO GOOD
> STARTED MAKING TROUBLE IN THE NEIGHBOURHOOD
> AND VERY SOON SOMETHING HAPPENED WHICH WAS TOTALLY WEIRD:
> THE KING AND QUEEN OF COLCHESTER BOTH DISAPPEARED.

That's right - the Queen's sister, was the evil and cruel villain Carabosse **(boo)**. And the royal baby, left with no mother and father, was our hero Princess Luna **(cheer)**. Ready for

---

[1] A licence issued to perform this play does not include permission to use the music specified in this copy.

chapter two? Here goes...

> BUT NEXT, LEAN FORWARD AND LISTEN
> CARABOSSE SAW THE CROWN JEWELS GLISTEN
> WITH LUNA, MERELY A BABY
> TAKING HER POWER WAS MORE THAN A MAYBE
> DID IT EVER STOP, YO? THAT'S A NO.
> HER EVIL AMBITION CONTINUED TO GROW
> THEN LATER ONE NIGHT IN THE DEPTHS OF THE WILD
> CARABOSSE ABANDONED THE CHILD

But fortunately I saw Carabosse up to no good and secretly saved Baby Luna from her terrible plight. I took her to two friends of mine, Dame Maris Piper and her son Spud, who have hidden and protected Luna from her wicked Aunt, Queen Carabosse. Fortunately for the last eighteen years, Luna...

Grown up LUNA appears through the gauze.

...has grown up to be generous, kind-hearted, and the true spirit of this wonderful city, but she has no idea of her royal heritage. Carabosse on the other hand, unaware that her niece is still alive, abuses her use of the royal sceptre on a daily basis and is even more of a tyrant than before.

(RAPPER'S DELIGHT:)

> NOW WHAT YOU HEAR, IS NOT A JOKE,
> I'M RISING TO THE TEST.
> AND SOON, IN TIME,
> YOU FRIENDS OF MINE
> WILL FIND OUT WHO'S THE BEST.
> SEE I AM FAIRY-FIZZ,
> AND HERE'S WHAT I'VE GOT SAY
> DON'T MESS WITH ME
> OR CAUSE STRESS FOR ME

BECAUSE WE ARE GONNA WIN THE DAY
BUT FIRST WE GOTTA:
BANG BANG THE BOOGIE TO THE BOOGIE
SAY UP JUMP THE BOOGIE TO THE BANG BANG
BOOGIE
LET'S ROCK, YOU DON'T STOP
ROCK THE RHYTHM THAT'LL MAKE YOUR BODY ROCK
AGAIN

F to the I to the Zed Zed why? She's Fizzy!
(Whoop! Whoop!)
She's Fizzy! Oh yeah.

F to the I to the Zed Zed why? She's Fizzy!
(Whoop! Whoop!)
She's Fizzy! Oh yeah.

Yo yo yo, thanks gang. To defeat Carabozza we just need to get Luna to her 18th birthday in 2 days time! I feel a celebration coming on around here … Let's get LOUD!

Music as the cloth flies out to reveal ..

Scene 2 - Town Square

Song: *Welcome to the Village / There's Gonna be a Party*

As FAIRY FIZZ sings, LUNA and TOWNSFOLK start dressing the town square with party decorations.

SONG: 'There's Gonna be a Party.'
(FIZZ, LUNA & TOWNSFOLK)

After song -

LUNA
(To Audience) Hello everybody! **(Hello)** My name's Luna and it's so awesome that you're all here with me: because in two days time it's my birthday party and you're all invited.

TOWNSFOLK
Hooray!

FAIRY FIZZ
We can't wait, Luna. Your birthday is just what everyone needs to lift their spirits.

LUNA
Thanks Fizz. My Mum keeps telling me I have to keep it low key but what's the point in celebrating if it isn't with all my friends. *(To audience)* Hey do you lot want to be my friends? **(Yes)** Amazing!

TOWNS PERSON 1
Everyone loves a good party, don't they?

TOWNSFOLK
Yeah! *Etc.*

FAIRY-FIZZ
Everyone except you know who.

LUNA
Who?!

ALL TOWNSFOLK
Queen Carabosse...

LUNA
I've never met her, but she sounds like a right moodypants.

TOWNS PERSON 2
She's been raising the rents again.

TOWNS PERSON 3
And threatening to do terrible things if we don't pay up.

TOWNS PERSON 1
We couldn't pay up last week, so she made my cat go woof!

LUNA
I don't believe that. Cats can't go woof.

TOWNS PERSON 1
It did when she set fire to it. Woof!

FAIRY-FIZZ
In that case you better get back to work or she'll have
everyone evicted.

TOWNSFOLK
Bye/See you tomorrow/Bye Luna etc.

LUNA
Bye everyone, see you at the party!

   The TOWNSFOLK exit.

LUNA
Oh Fizz, I thought that turning eighteen might give me some
freedom but Mum's stricter than ever. She's always worrying.
Telling me 'not to talk to strangers' and to 'be home by 7
o'clock' every night.

FAIRY-FIZZ
There are some dangerous people out there, Luna. You heard
what they said about Queen Carabosse.

LUNA
Yeah she sounds super gloomy - who would want to be Queen
if it made you as mean as Carabosse?

FAIRY-FIZZ
Royals can't always chose to be royals, Luna.

LUNA
But they can chose how to use their power! *(Laughing at the
idea)* If I were Queen - we'd have a party everyday and no
one would have to pay rent at all!

FAIRY-FIZZ
        (With a knowing look to the audience)
Sounds perfect to me. I'll see you later Luna.

LUNA
Bye Fizz!

        FIZZ exits. Underscore.

(To Audience) Now then everyone, I need your help. My best
friend Polo keeps running off. He's a bit of an explorer you
see, so will you lot help me find him? **(Yes)** Will you? **(Yes)**
Ah thanks - okay if you see Polo you've got to shout out really
loudly and tell me where he is. I'll have a quick look over
here.

As LUNA heads DSR. POLO the penguin pops out from USR and crosses to DSL. The audience shout out as music plays.

Where is he? **(He's over there!)** Is he over here? **(No, no, over there)** Oh - over here. **(Yes)** OK I'll have another look.

As LUNA heads DSL. POLO pops out from USL and crosses to DSR. The audience shout out as music plays.

What - he's over there now? **(Yes!)** Listen you'll have to be much louder when you see him. **(He's there! He's there!)**

POLO plays Peek A Boo around LUNA, and eventually jumps out at her.

POLO
Llelooo! *('Hello')*

> **POLO speaks a kind of Pingu language. It is fully intentioned and nearly understandable, but the words are not English. POLO is everyone's best friend, but only LUNA fully understands his speech.*

LUNA
There you are Polo - you little mischief-maker. Hey, do you want to meet my new friends?

He looks at them to suss them out, but decides against it.

POLO
Urrrr Llo Llankoo! *('Errrr No thank you')*

LUNA
Hey that's very rude, what's wrong with my new friends?

He looks at them, sniffs them, signals that they smell funny and turns away.

POLO
LLaylar llelly sllelly (*'They are very smelly'*)

LUNA
Don't worry, boys and girls, he's playing hard to get, so we'll just have to try extra hard to be friends with him. So after 3, I want everyone to shout 'Hello Polo'. Ready 1,2,3? **(Hello Polo).**

Nothing.

We're gonna have to try harder than that I think, 1, 2, 3 **(Hello Polo)**

POLO starts to walk away.

Oh no he's really playing hard to get - one more time as loud as you can 1, 2, 3 **(Hello Polo!)**.

POLO a dances a brief musical line.

POLO
Llelooo! (*'Hello'*)

LUNA
Now come on Polo, we better get stuff sorted for the party. We'll be back shortly, friends, bye!

LUNA and POLO exit.

Entrance music, as SPUD PIPER enters on a scooter. He doesn't stop. Crash!

SPUD
Hello everybody - yes it's me, back by public transport, and my name's Spud - Spud Piper - and I work for my Mum's food delivery business. But oh dear everyone, she's such a bad cook she uses the smoke alarm as a timer. Honestly, in our house we pray *after* the meal. Cordon bleu? Should be cordoned off. To be honest, she's the main cook and I'm her sous chef. Which means that when I cook we get sued. Hey do you wanna be in my gang? When I come on, I'm gonna shout 'Alright kids?' And I want you lot to shout back 'Alright Spud' - will you do that for me? **(Yes!)** Great - let's give it a go then. Alright kids **(Alright Spud)** I said Alright Kids **(Alright Spud)**, Alright left side!**(Alright Spud)** Alright right side! **(Alright Spud)**. That's brilliant, thanks guys.-Now I live with my mum, Maris Piper, and my two best friends, Luna and Polo. But guess what? **(What?)** I said guess what? **(What?)** We're really poor **(Aaah)**. And we can't pay the rent **(Aaah)**. But worst of all, kids, guess what? **(What?)** I haven't got a girlfriend **(Aaahhh)**. I've been on so many first dates, you know?
One girl was very rude - Kirsten Swore.
Another wanted me to sing to her - Sarah Nader
And another spent the whole date juggling cans of lager - Beatrix.
One girl left and went to Africa - Rhoda Camel
One left and went to L.A - Holly Wood
And another left and went to a toilet in Serbia - Ivana Tinkle.

  SFX of motorbike revs.

Uh oh. I think that's my Mum, I'm getting out of here. See you later gang!

  Entrance music, as DAME MARIS PIPER enters on the back of a Deliveroo-esque scooter.

MARIS
Hello Colchester. **(Hello)**. I said Hello Colchester! **(Hello!)**. Oh look at you all, don't you all look gorgeous. It's like the grand opening party for the new Greggs. And you've all dressed-up for the occasion. I'm not sure what as, but you've all dressed up.

> *She bangs her chest and coughs out smoke (through a clenched fist of talc).*

Now that's better: my name's Dame Maris Piper and I've just launched my new food delivery business - It's called Maris Piper's Meals On Heels.

> *Riffs...*

I live in a little cottage, in a little forest, on a large stage, in a large theatre. I live with my son Spud, our pet Penguin Polo and I've been looking after Princess Luna since she was a baby. She's not a baby anymore though. Now she's nearly 18 and all she wants is a big birthday party which I'd love to give her but I cannot let Queen Carabosse find out she's alive. I've been trying to protect her since her parents disappeared all those years ago.

Now talking of a tragedy - *(SFX loud 'TRAGEDY')* - I must tell you: I've had a trying morning **(Aaah)**. It was more trying than that **(Aaah)**. It was a little-less-sarcastic-and-slightly-more-sincerely trying than that **(AAAH)** - That's how trying it was. It all started when I was driving down the A12, I got distracted by a Marmite van heading yeast-bound, and I crashed into a lorry full of onions and had to find a hard shoulder to cry on. What a tragedy - *(SFX loud 'TRAGEDY')*.

But you lot will help cheer me up because every time I come on I'm going to say 'Hi-de-hi folks', and I want you all to shout back 'Ho-de-ho Maris'! Will you do that for me? **(Yes)** I said 'Will you'? **(Yes)**. Alright let's give it a go: Hi-de-hi folks!

(Ho-de-ho Maris), we can do better than that, I said 'Hi-de-hi folks!' **(Ho-de-ho Maris!)**. Just the kids in the house 'Hi-de-hi boys and girls **(Ho-de-ho Maris)**, all my fellow ladies in the house 'Hi-de-hi ladies' **(Ho-de-ho Maris!)** And finally all the dads, uncles and grandads in the house 'Hi-de-hi gentlemen' **(Ho-de-ho Maris)**. Oh ladies - that may sound like a load of bored blokes who've been dragged along to the local pantomime, but no! No! That is the unmistakable sound of nature's masculine embodiments looking for lurrrve.

Funky sexy underscore plays as the lights come up FOH and Maris heads into the audience.

Now look at you wild creatures. This gentleman here spent so long doing his hair he left it at home. Oh and look - two men 'too sexy for their hair'- sitting right next to each other. Oh no it's a lady in a low cut top. Sorry madam. But wait a minute!!

Eastenders drum fill and record scratch SFX.

Hello stud-muffin. Stand up, tiger. I may not have a library card but I'm happy to check you out. What's your name, cupcake? **(Graham)** Graham? Graham! What a heroic name, Graham. And where are you from, Graham? **(Icklesham)** I'm sorry? **(Icklesham)** No I heard you the first time I'm just sorry. I had a feeling you might come after me, heroic Graham, so I'm wearing my Colchester football club bra. No cups and very little support. But in this bra heroic Graham, is my personal hanky, made of perfect girlfriend material, **(*Handing over hanky and heading back onstage*)** and every time I say 'Hi-de-di Graham', I want you to wave this hanky frantically in the air and shout back 'Ho-de-ho Maris'. Will you do that for me? Oh thank you Graham. Let's give it a go then: 'Hi-de-hi Graham'. **(Ho-de-ho Maris)**. Oh wonderful. To think I was single and ready to mingle, and now my dingle's beginning to tingle. Do you know what, Graham? I have a feeling that tonight will be a night you'll never forget.

SONG: Maris is Hot for [Graham]!
(MARIS PIPER and her FLAMING CHORUS.)

> _At the end of the number, the FLAMING CHORUS spell
> out the name of MARIS' new boyfriend._

What do you think about that, Graham? As my mother would
say, always leave them wanting less.

> _Play out as FLAMING CHORUS exit and SPUD enters._

SPUD
Alright kids **(Alright Spud)** I said Alright Kids **(Alright
Spud).** Blimey mum, you've put on a few pounds.

MARIS
Well I've had a lot on my plate.

SPUD
Is that a new hat?

MARIS
Yes, I was down in the dumps so I got myself a new one.

SPUD
I wondered where you found it.

MARIS
Don't be mean.

SPUD
But I love what you've done with your hair. How do you get it
to come out your nostrils like that?

MARIS

You cheeky thing.

SPUD
Actually, mum, in a certain light you are as beautiful as
Barbie.

MARIS
(Adjusting her angle) Ooh thank you - what light's that?

> *Blackout.*

You cheeky monkey!

> *Lights up.*

I have worked my fingers to the bone for you, and what have
I got to show for it?

SPUD
Boney fingers?

MARIS
You're so lazy you never do nothing for me. You're a Sofa
Spud. And why do I call you a Sofa Spud?

SPUD
Cause I'm a couch potato.

MARIS
That's right. I'm always left to do everything myself - and I
have been a widow since your father died in child birth.

SPUD
Do you miss him?

MARIS
I do. I remember I used to rub grease all over his back to
make him feel better.

SPUD
What happened?

MARIS
He went downhill very quickly.

SPUD
Hey Mum...

MARIS
What?

SPUD
I've just heard that because Colchester's got city status,
Queen Carabosse is coming for a royal visit.

MARIS
Oh my goodness, this is a travesty.

>   *SFX 'Tragedy'*

>   *(to sound desk)*
I said Travesty not Tragedy. Honestly, how many times did we
rehearse this?

>   *SFX 'Is It Too Late Now To Say Sorry?'*

>   *(to sound desk)*
Yes it is. Funny way to hand in your notice.
>   *(to SPUD)*
Where were we?

SPUD
Queen Carabosse is going to be coming here in person.

MARIS
Oh my goodness, this is a tragedy… *(to sound desk)* too late,
missed it!… *(to Spud)* We must get Luna home before
Carabosse sees her.

LUNA and POLO enter with the TOWNSFOLK.

LUNA
Hi Mum. Hi Spud.

MARIS
There you both are. Hello everyone.

TOWNSFOLK
Hello!

MARIS
Now Luna, I need you to go to Coggeshall immediately, to
pick up some butter for me?

LUNA
Butter? I just got you some.

MARIS
Well get me some more. *(A warning to Luna)* But wait a
minute. Before you go anywhere: Spud, what is my favourite
saying?

SPUD
'You can lead a horse to water but a pencil must be lead'

MARIS
Not that one.

SPUD
'Some say their body's a temple but mine's a bouncy castle.'

MARIS
Not that one.

SPUD
'Roses are red
Violets are purple
Poems are hard
Wibbly wurple'

MARIS
Spud! My favourite saying is:

MARIS & SPUD
'Stay out of trouble!'

SPUD
Oh *that* one.

LUNA
How could I forget? But really what is there to be worried about?

    Evil sting

CARABOSSE enters. Everyone kneels, except SPUD.

CARABOSSE
I am the great and powerful Queen of this realm and as controller of the Royal Sceptre... Excuse me, your Queen is here, kneel!

SPUD
Hello Neil, lovely to meet you.

CARABOSSE
I didn't mean that. I mean you! Kneel!

SPUD
No, I'm Spud Piper.

CARABOSSE
Bend down!

SPUD
No, Spud Piper. That's Ben Down over there. Say hello Ben.

TOWNS PERSON BEN
Hello

CARABOSSE
Lower!

SPUD
(lower pitch) Say hello Ben.

TOWNS PERSON BEN
(lower pitch) Hello

CARABOSSE
Bend down, on one knee.

SPUD
He is on one knee.

CARABOSSE
Not him - *(h')*you!

SPUD
Hugh's on one knee as well. Say hello, Hugh.

TOWNS PERSON HUGH
Hello

CARABOSSE
I'm waiting! 3 - 2 - 1

MARIS pulls SPUD down just in time and whispers to him.

SPUD
Oh!

CARABOSSE
Hmm, just in time.

SPUD
No that's Justin over there, say hello Justin -

STAGE MANAGER JUSTIN
(entering with headphones and clipboard) Hiya

He exits

CARABOSSE
Silence! What's that smell? Balloons! Balloons equal parties, parties equal pleasure, pleasure equals leisure, leisure equals too much money - time to hike up the rents.

LUNA
I don't think you understand, these balloons are for -

MARIS
Spud! They're for Spud. To remember when he worked at the Helium Factory - he took them with him when he left.

CARABOSSE
Why did you leave?

SPUD
I wasn't gonna let them speak to me like that.

LUNA
They're actually for me Queen Carabosse.

CARABOSSE
You? Who are you?

LUNA
I'm Luna /

MARIS
-TIC!

CARABOSSE
What?

MARIS
She's a lunatic.

SPUD
Completely batty.

MARIS
We try to remind her to -

MARIS and SPUD
(Spelling it out) Stay out of trouble.

LUNA
I was just saying my name. My name is -

MARIS
Graham!

SPUD
Graham! (To MARIS) Graham?

MARIS
(taking Luna to the side) That's right. Stand over here,
Graham, you lunatic, and

SPUD and MARIS
Stay. Out. Of. Trouble!

SPUD
(to CARABOSSE) Very silly is Graham. Completely
unpredictable. If you've got any questions, Queen Carabosse,
best to come through me.

CARABOSSE
What are these balloons for?!

LUNA
They're for my birthday party, Queen Carabosse.

    MARIS and SPUD intake of breath.

CARABOSSE
Birthday party?

LUNA
You see I'm going to be eighteen in two days.

    MARIS and SPUD intake of breath.

CARABOSSE
Eighteen? In two days?

LUNA
And everyone's looking forward to it.

    MARIS and SPUD intake of breath.

CARABOSSE
Everyone?

LUNA

Everyone. I hope you'll come too. My name's Luna by the way.

LUNA beams at CARABOSSE. The rumbling crescendos. Freeze.

CARABOSSE
(to us) Luna!? Eighteen? In two days?! It can't be?! She can't be!?

Unfreeze.

Colchester! I have a proclamation!

A scroll of paper magically appears in her hand.

(to Spud) You! Read it for me.

SPUD
Yes boss Carabosse. *(Reading it)* To the people of Colchester, from today, all celebrations are banned across the land including the land on the grand band stand. Anyone found even mentioning the words 'Happy'-

CARABOSSE
(an instinctive reaction) Aah!

SPUD
- or 'Birthday' -

CARABOSSE
Ooh!

SPUD
That's 'Happy' -

CARABOSSE
Aah!

SPUD
- or 'Birthday' -

CARABOSSE
Ooh!

SPUD
How about 'Happy Birthday'?

CARABOSSE
Aah ooh!

SPUD
Or 'Birthday Happy'?

CARABOSSE
Ooh aah!

SPUD
What about 'Happy-Birthday-Birth-Birth-Happy'?

CARABOSSE
Ooh-ee-ooh-ah-ah!

ALL
Ting-tang-walla-walla-bing-bang!

CARABOSSE
Read it!

SPUD
Anyone found saying these words will receive a severe
punishment.

LUNA
This is ridiculous. You can't do this, Queen Carabosse,
tomorrow is my 18th b-

23

MARIS
Luna!

LUNA
What have I done to upset you? You don't have to come along
if you don't want to.

MARIS
Luna!

LUNA
(Calmer) What's wrong with celebrating, Carabosse?

> *Ominous Music. CARABOSSE goes around popping
> balloons.*

CARABOSSE
Let me be very clear. There shall be no celebrations of any
kind in two days time. And if I see anybody even
acknowledging this child's eighteenth...thingy, you'll all be out
on the streets before you can say... *(She teases them about to
popping a final balloon. She doesn't)* Bang... Aren't needles
fun?!

> *CARABOSSE exits as all the remaining balloons pop.*

MARIS
Now look what you've done, Luna. What did I say to you?

LUNA
You said stay out of trouble. Inviting her to my party is hardly
making trouble.

MARIS
But Carabosse controls the Royal Sceptre.

SPUD
Which makes everyone miserable, 'cept her.

MARIS
We're ruined. Ruined! If she puts up the rent again we won't
be able to afford it. We're going to lose everything, I'll be flat
broke and homeless.

LUNA
Mum! Listen, nobody's ruined here. And nobody's going to be
ruined if we all stick together. We may not have much money
but we've all got each other, right? With each other, we're
richer than Queen Carabosse will ever be.

SONG: We Must Stick Together!

> *LUNA, SPUD, MARIS AND TOWNSFOLK try to cheer
> themselves up.*

> *After song -*

MARIS
Oh that has cheered me up love. Thank you. Now take Polo to
Coggeshall and get me that butter. We best get back to work
before Carabosse returns.

Scene 3 - The Forest

Musical sting - Immigrant Song Ahh Ahhh -
CARABOSSE enters, brandishing the royal sceptre.

CARABOSSE
Boo boo boo. Go on, get it out of your system, let's have one
big 'hiss' at me: 1,2,3 **(Hiss)**. Haha you've all got spit on
you. Look at you. You're all so ugly, if you went to a Haunted
house they'd give you job application forms. So. Baby Luna,
back from the dead. Who does she think she is?! Coming back
to haunt me after eighteen years of ultimate power. But as
controller of the Royal Sceptre, I set the rules around here,
and nobody will get in my way.

Flash. Musical flourish. FAIRY-FIZZ enters.

FAIRY-FIZZ
F to the I to the Zed Zed why? She's Fizzy!
(Whoop! Whoop!)
She's Fizzy! Oh yeah.
Ya killing it folks, that's mega. Not so fast Queen Carabosse.
You may have had eighteen unchallenged years on the throne
but things are about to change. Luna has grown up to be
generous, kind-hearted, and more populizzle than you'll ever
be.

CARABOSSE
I'll soon put an end to that mangy toe-rag. I've got a secret
idea brewing (*miming touching a spinning wheel*) which I
can't quite 'put my finger' on at the moment, and if any of
you lot try to stop me, I'll poison your interval ice creams.

Music. She exits.

FAIRY-FIZZ
Carabosse is never gettin' past us lot. She may have found
out about Luna being alive, but as long as we keep her out of

harms way, she'll be fine. But now it's time to shake things up...

PRINCE ISTUNA appears through the gauze.

...This is Istuna, the Prince of Coggeshall. Remember, Luna's on her way to pick up some butter. I think she might find more than she was expecting - ya get me?

FAIRY-FIZZ exits.
PRINCE ISTUNA is joined by his advisor TIMOTHY.

TIMOTHY
Your royal highness, the bunting's up, the tents are pitched, and the archery is ready to go.

PRINCE
Isn't it a bit excessive for a first date?

TIMOTHY
Excessive? No, sir. Your father, the King, insists you marry into royalty, so your chances of finding someone he approves of are very slim. Hence why I created a profile for you on the royal dating app, Sovereign Soulmates.

PRINCE
Oh I hate this royal dating stuff, why can't I marry whoever I want to?

TIMOTHY
(handing him a card) I really think this is the one, sir.

PRINCE
(reading) 5 ft 8, Fingringhoe.

TIMOTHY
Her location.

PRINCE
Of course. Beautiful, kind, generous, fun-loving, likes a spot
of archery, allergic to peanut butter. GSOH.

TIMOTHY
Good sense of humour.

PRINCE
NMNK

TIMOTHY
Never married, no kids.

PRINCE
No ONS.

TIMOTHY
She's looking for a soul mate sir.

PRINCE
When is she arriving?

TIMOTHY
Imminently.

PRINCE
Right, you better teach me how to shoot an arrow then.

TIMOTHY
Very good sir.

	They exit as LUNA and POLO enter.

LUNA
Well here we are, Polo: Coggeshall. Gosh look at this place:
that's gentrification for you. I wonder if Prince Istuna is
around.

POLO
Dloo Lluuur dim. *('You lurrrrve him')*

LUNA
Polo, I do not love the Prince, I've only ever seen pictures of
him. I'd like to meet him IRL and... and talk to him, and...
and -

POLO
('Kiss him and squeeze him and do sexy dancing together.')

LUNA
No I do not want to do that. Polo stop it, that's ridiculous.
Alright that's enough!

     POLO stops.

Okay maybe I do like him a little, but if he was here now I'd
be as cool as a cucumber -

     PRINCE ISTUNA enters.

PRINCE
That's that sorted.

LUNA
(Privately to Polo) Holy Mackrel that's him!

PRINCE
(Privately to Timothy) Sheesh kebabs that's her!

POLO
(Privately to Luna) Dleet dlarm!

TIMOTHY
(Privately to the Prince) Keep calm!

POLO
An Lleelemba -

TIMOTHY
And remember -

POLO
Dairs Lludding d' dloooo.

TIMOTHY
(Identical) Dairs Lludding d' dloooo.

PRINCE
What?

TIMOTHY
There's nothing to loooose.

> *Simultaneously, TIMOTHY and POLO turn the Prince and Luna respectively and push them towards each other. POLO and TIMOTHY pretend to be busy.*

PRINCE
Hello.

LUNA
Hello.

PRINCE
I'm very well thank you, how are you?

LUNA
Erm, I'm very well thank you.

PRINCE
(Miming a bow and arrow) Do you play Archery often?

LUNA
I'm sorry?

PRINCE
(Miming a bow and arrow) Do you, does one, do Archery
often?

LUNA
Erm -

PRINCE
Don't worry we've hidden the Peanut Butter!

LUNA
Excuse me?

PRINCE
You're welcome - lovely to meet you.

LUNA
You too.

> The PRINCE and LUNA turn to their respective
> advisors...

PRINCE
This is going terribly.

LUNA
He's - kind of goofy.

> *...and turn back.*

PRINCE
Sorry I should introduce myself. I am Prince Istuna of
Coggeshall.

LUNA
Oh I know I've been watching you.

PRINCE
Watching me?

LUNA
I mean I've been looking at pictures of you.

PRINCE
Pictures of me?

LUNA
Pictures of your face - FLAGS! Your flags. I love your flags!

PRINCE
My flags.

LUNA
You're welcome - lovely to meet you.

PRINCE
You too.

> The PRINCE and LUNA turn to their respective
> advisors...

LUNA
This is going terribly.

PRINCE
She's - kind of weird.

> ...and turn back.

LUNA
Sorry I should introduce *myself*. I'm Luna, I live in a small
cottage in Colchester.

PRINCE
Oh. You're not the err -

LUNA
The what?

PRINCE
5ft 8, Fingringhoe...

LUNA
Excuse me?

PRINCE
From Sovereign Soulmates.

LUNA
No.

PRINCE
"Beautiful, kind, generous, fun-loving, likes a spot of archery, allergic to peanut butter."

LUNA
Definitely not me.

PRINCE
Oh.

LUNA
I *love* peanut butter.

        Prince laughs. Music in.

PRINCE
Me too.

LUNA
Archery?

PRINCE
Can't stand it.

LUNA
Me neither. I prefer boxing.

SONG: I Really Like This Person!
(PRINCE and LUNA)

> *TIMOTHY and POLO get caught up in the romantic duet.*
>
> *Song. Before final chorus -*

LUNA
Got any plans tomorrow evening?

PRINCE
Not at the moment, why do you ask?

LUNA
It's my birthday party, you could be my date.

PRINCE
I thought I was supposed to ask you out first?

LUNA
You'd probably get all tongue-tied and ask me to play archery again. I'm not taking any chances. It's tomorrow evening. I'll send you an invite.

PRINCE
All right, see you then.

> *Final chorus of song.*

Song ends. LUNA points at something and the PRINCE turns to it.

She kisses him on the cheek and runs off.

Play out. The PRINCE exits the other way as the cloth goes out.

Scene 4 - Maris's Kitchen

MARIS
Hi-di-hi folks **(Ho-de-ho Maris).** Hi-di-hi Graham **(Ho-de-ho Maris).** Welcome to my home everybody! I've lived here 50 years man and boy and I know what you're thinking, it's very big for a poor lady like me, but let me tell you, it was like magic (*SFX loud* 'MAGIC')! Not a Tragedy (*SFX loud* 'TRAGEDY') - but like magic (*SFX loud* 'MAGIC')! I fell asleep one evening, dreaming that a big, strong builder might come and lay my patio, and I woke up with a huge extension.

   SPUD enters.

SPUD
Alright kids! **(Alright Spud!)** Morning, Mum.

MARIS
Morning, Spud. Now, Spud, can you keep a secret?

SPUD
I can keep a secret, it's the people I tell them to who can't.

MARIS
Well, with Luna's birthday party cancelled we've got to find a way to keep her happy and hidden at home. So I am secretly making her an especially special, secret birthday cake! **(Oooh!).** But remember, we mustn't let Queen Carabosse find out.

SPUD
Righto mum. But if no one comes to Luna's birthday party...?

MARIS
She can have her cake and eat it too. Now then it's all very simple, Spud. I read out the recipe and deliver the ingredients, you put them in the bowl and mix it all around.

SPUD
Read out the recipe - deliver the ingredients - put them in the
bowl - mix it all around.

MARIS
Baker - are you ready?

SPUD
Mother - I am ready.

MARIS
3,2,1 bake.

SONG: BAKE A CAKE
(MARIS and SPUD)

> *Routine to the tune of 'There was an old lady who
> swallowed a fly'*

MARIS
NOW THIS IS THE MIXTURE FOR BAKIN' A CAKE
WHADDYA SAY, SHALL WE BAKE A CAKE?

SPUD
LET'S BAKE A CAKE.

MARIS
NOW FIRST ON THE LIST IS WE NEED THE CREAM
AND WHIP IT AND FLIP IT TO TASTE LIKE A DREAM

> *8 counts: MARIS swishes around a bucket of slosh near
> the bowl, but puts it in the bowl.*

FOR THIS IS THE MIXTURE FOR BAKIN' A CAKE
WHADDYA SAY, SHALL WE BAKE A CAKE?

SPUD
LET'S BAKE A CAKE.

MARIS
NOW NEXT ON THE LIST IS WE NEED AN EGG

SPUD
WE NEED AN EGG? THEN THROW US AN EGG!

> *8 counts: Maris throws the egg and SPUD catches it in the bowl (drum roll, slide whistle and triangle)*

MARIS
AND NEXT ON THE LIST IS WE NEED THE CREAM AND WHIP
IT AND FLIP IT TO TASTE LIKE A DREAM

> *This time MARIS' slosh swishing is a little less controlled.*

FOR THIS IS THE MIXTURE FOR BAKIN' A CAKE
WHADDYA SAY, SHALL WE BAKE A CAKE?

SPUD
LET'S BAKE A CAKE.

MARIS
NOW NEXT ON THE LIST IS WE NEED SOME MILK
A SPLATTER WILL MAKE IT AS SMOOTH AS SILK

> *8 counts: MARIS heads over with a carton of milk.*

Can you just double check this hasn't gone off?

> *SPUD smells, MARIS squeezes the carton and the milk squirts in his face. Each time the ingredients are repeated, the egg is thrown, the slosh swished, the milk squirted etc. with decreasing accuracy and increasing mess.*

AND NEXT ON THE LIST IS WE NEED AN EGG
AND NEXT ON THE LIST IS WE NEED THE CREAM

AND WHIP IT AND FLIP IT TO TASTE LIKE A DREAM
FOR THIS IS THE MIXTURE FOR BAKIN' A CAKE
WHADDYA SAY, SHALL WE BAKE A CAKE?

SPUD
LET'S BAKE A CAKE.

MARIS
NOW NEXT ON THE LIST IS WE NEED SOME WATER
Polo! Spud, would like some water!

> *8 counts: POLO enters with a water pistol and fires
> directly at SPUD.*

AND NEXT ON THE LIST IS WE NEED SOME MILK
AND NEXT ON THE LIST IS WE NEED AN EGG
AND NEXT ON THE LIST IS WE NEED THE CREAM
AND WHIP IT AND FLIP IT TO TASTE LIKE A DREAM
FOR THIS IS THE MIXTURE FOR BAKIN' A CAKE
WHADDYA SAY, SHALL WE BAKE A CAKE?

SPUD
IT'S A FUNNY OLD CAKE

MARIS
NOW NEXT ON THE LIST IS YOU NEED A PIE
THE THING WITH A PIE IS IT COMES FROM THE SKY.

> *8 counts*

SPUD
What do you mean it comes from the Sky?

> *SPUD looks to the sky and MARIS puts a pie in his face.*

MARIS
AND NEXT ON THE LIST IS WE NEED SOME WATER
AND NEXT ON THE LIST IS WE NEED SOME MILK

AND NEXT ON THE LIST IS WE NEED AN EGG
AND NEXT ON THE LIST IS WE NEED THE CREAM
AND WHIP IT AND FLIP IT TO TASTE LIKE A DREAM
FOR THIS IS THE MIXTURE FOR BAKIN' A CAKE
WHADDYA SAY, DID WE BAKE A CAKE?

SPUD
I NEED A BREAK

MARIS
NOW NEXT ON THE LIST IS WE NEED A TOWEL

SPUD
A TOWEL? A TOWEL? I'D LOVE A TOWEL?

> *MARIS throws SPUD the towel over his head. As he
> turns. POLO is waiting with a pie and water. Carnage
> ensures.*

AND NEXT ON THE LIST IS WE NEED A PIE
AND NEXT ON THE LIST IS WE NEED SOME WATER
AND NEXT ON THE LIST IS WE NEED SOME MILK
AND NEXT ON THE LIST IS WE NEED AN EGG
AND NEXT ON THE LIST IS WE NEED THE CREAM
AND WHIP IT AND FLIP IT TO TASTE LIKE A DREAM
FOR THIS IS THE MIXTURE FOR BAKIN' A CAKE
WHADDYA SAY?
WHADDYA SAY?
WHADDYA SAY?
SHALL WE BAKE A CAAAAKE?

SPUD
FOR GOODNESS SAKE.

> *Music out. Applause. Music in, slowly, as if there's
> more.*

MARIS
NOW LAST ON THE LIST IS YOU GIVE IT A KISS

SPUD
GIVE IT A KISS?! YOU'RE TAKING THE -

> *SFX Loud ominous knocking.*

MARIS and SPUD
Carabosse!

MARIS
(shocked) Oh no! Quick! Hide everything! She can't know
what we've been up to or she'll evict us!

> *Music. Chaos ensues as they all try and clear everything
> as fast as possible.*

Polo, run and turn the lights off. We'll pretend we're out.

> *Blackout, whilst the tarpaulin and mess is whipped away
> super quickly replaced by nothing but a giant, tiered
> birthday cake with a large candle on the top in the
> middle. Lights up.*

LUNA
(Off) Spud? Mum? Polo? I'm home! *(Entering)* Oh wow!

MARIS
Oh thank goodness it's you, Luna, we thought you were
Carabosse. Yeah and we were making a complete mess of
your -

> *They spot the cake.*

MARIS, LUNA & POLO
WHAAAAAH?!!

LUNA
Did you make this for me, Mum? I'm amazed!

MARIS
You're amazed? I'm *astounded*!

LUNA
It's ginormous!

SPUD
That'll be the 17 eggs.

LUNA
I think I might cry.

SPUD
The cake's already in tiers.

LUNA
It's the best present ever, it can't get any better than this!

MARIS & SPUD
Happy Birthday, Luna!

> *Bang. Evil music. CARABOSSE appears out of the middle of the cake, wearing the candle as a hat.*

CARABOSSE
What did you say?!

LUNA
It's you!

CARABOSSE
It's me!

MARIS
(*petrified*) Your majesty!

SPUD
(*petrified*) Carrabossyboots!

CARABOSSE
Isn't my arrival just the icing on the cake? I was hiding inside
here -

MARIS
As you do.

CARABOSSE
- and I heard the two words you are forbidden to speak!
(Pointing at Spud) You - what have I said before about
celebrations?

SPUD
I LIKE BIG CAKES AND I CANNOT LIE

CARABOSSE
Not *that* one.

SPUD
'Roses are red
Violets are blue
If you hide in a cake
You smell like poo'

MARIS
Spud!

CARABOSSE
I *said...* there will be no celebrations in this town, *(towards
Maris and Spud)* and anyone who even *mentions* those two
words will have me to deal with.

> Each time she hears these words, CARABOSSE has an
> instinctive vocal reaction which grows in horror. For

LUNA
In that case, Queen Carabosse, I'm very sorry that Maris and
Spud have upset you, but because it's my birthday / they
were saying Happy Birthday / to happy me / for my birthday /
because we're all happy / and it is my birthday /. And I don't
care about your stupid rules because everyone thinks you're
wicked and mean and cruel and horrible so 'Happy Birthday'-
on-my-Birthday-makes-me-happy!

CARABOSSE
STOOOOP!

Music rumble. Lightening flashes.

MARIS
Oh no.

CARABOSSE
You had to push me over the edge didn't you? You think you
know everything, you think you're so popular, you think
you're so 'good'. You're just a stroppy little teenager who
can't obey the rules.

LUNA
And you're a plain old bully, Carabosse.

CARABOSSE
NO! I'm not a plain old bully, I'm a *powerful* bully. And I'm
raising the rents on this cottage.

MARIS
Again?!

SPUD

Oh no!

CARABOSSE
If you don't have ten thousand pounds by tomorrow morning,
you'll be out on the streets with immediate effect.

>   *Bang. Music. She exits.*

SPUD
(As if she were still in the room) Yeah well if you don't stop
being such a meany by tomorrow morning, I'll - I'll - I'll still
be really scared.

MARIS
(to Luna) Are you happy now?

LUNA
It's about time she knew what people thought of her.

MARIS
Oh well that's fine. Spud and I, we'll just pack our bags and
sleep in the gutter but at least Carabosse will know what you
think of her.

LUNA
We can't let her ruin our lives like that.

MARIS
Well you just did. And you can kiss goodbye to any birthday
celebrations.

LUNA
Never mind my birthday. What about Carabosse? I'm going to
tell everyone in Colchester to stand up to her.

MARIS
You'll do nothing of the sort, it's past 7 o'clock.

LUNA
I'm nearly eighteen, Mum, I can make my own decisions.

MARIS
Not in this house you can't. You're under my roof, you'll do as
I say.

LUNA
Then I wish I lived under a different roof.

	Beat.

MARIS
Well if that's how you feel then you'd better leave.

LUNA
(backtracking) I didn't mean it like that, Mum.

MARIS
I think you'd better go.

LUNA
I'll fix this I promise. I'll think of something.

MARIS
Just go.

	She leaves. POLO stays. Beat.

SPUD
Mum? ...Is now a good time to tell you I spent our last
remaining pennies on tickets to the local panto?*(No reply)*
They were pretty pricey as well. *(No reply)* Cracking cast
though apparently.

	He goes.

SONG: We Must Stick Together! *Reprise*
(Maris)

> *MARIS sings stoically to fight the tears. POLO watches from the door.*
>
> Then -
>
> *MARIS can't sing anymore. POLO comes and taps her on the shoulder. She turns.*
>
> *POLO gives her a big hug. The music swells, as the cloth falls and we segue to...*

Scene 5 - Forest

A dressmaker's wagon full of frocks, materials and mannequins.

CARABOSSE
Yes, yes, Boohoo. I've put my cunning plan into action. STEP ONE on the list to obtaining absolute power - suppress the rebels - tick! But naughty little Luna just couldn't stick to the rules. STEP TWO - divide your enemies - tick! Now that stupid potato family face a real potato famine, Luna will be on the streets before she can say triple cooked chips. Which leads me to STEP THREE - if there's someone standing in your way to absolute power, find a lovely, little, generous, kind and polite way... to GET RID OF THEM.

SONG: I Will Get What I Want!
(CARABOSSE / threaded through the following scene)

> Singing - then -

> *Music continues underneath.*

(Singing a la Disney princess) 'A seam is a stitch your cart makes'. Do you like my little travelling dress shop? It means that if any sad little girl would like a little dress to cheer them up they can come to me. Why me? Because I have scissors, and sharp needles, I know how to use them. Oh and with this disguise, nobody will suspect a thing. What can I say? I'm sexy and I sew it.

> *Sings -*

> *LUNA enters.*

LUNA
Oh friends, I really didn't mean to upset Maris, I just wish that Queen Carabosse didn't walk all over us. But I've had an

idea, I'm going to talk to the Prince - as a fellow royal he might be able to reason with Carabosse and make her see sense.

CARABOSSE pretends to be an OLD DRESSMAKER

CARABOSSE
(Singing as if to herself) 'I'm living in a material world, and I am a material girl'

LUNA
Oh how sweet, a travelling dressmaker in the forest. Hello!

CARABOSSE
(Singing as if to herself) 'Stitch me baby one more time'
Ah hello dear. Buy a new dress from a poor dear, dear?

LUNA
I'm sorry I can't afford one right now. Queen Carabosse has raised the rents and we've nothing left.

CARABOSSE
Oh dear, dear.

LUNA
She wants ten thousand pounds.

CARABOSSE
Dear-dear, dear, why so dear, dear?

LUNA
Well tomorrow is my birthday.

CARABOSSE
(styling it out) OOHHooh how sweet.

LUNA
And my best friends were caught saying 'Happy...

CARABOSSE
Ahh!

LUNA
...Birthday'.

CARABOSSE
Ooh!

LUNA
Everything ok?

CARABOSSE
Just feeling your pain dear. *(Moving to the cart)* But seeing as
your special day is coming up, I think this calls for a special
treat. Why don't you let me weave you a dress, entirely for
free, on my very special...magical...spinning wheel.

A magical spinning wheel comes downstage.

NEAT SEAMS ARE MADE OF THIS[2]
HOOK AND EYES, WHO'D DISAGREE?
TAILOR YOUR DREAMS WITH A SPINNING WHEEL
EVERYBODY'S LOOKING FOR SOMETHING

LUNA
Oh wow, I've never seen one of these before. Why is it so
magical?

CARABOSSE
If you touch the needle next to the wheel, it'll bring eternal
happiness to somebody close to you... Oh... and then it will
make you the dress of your dreams.

---

[2] Lyrics Based on 'Sweet Dreams Are Made of These'. A licence
issued to perform this play does not include permission to use the
music specified in this copy.

LUNA
Oh I don't know, I'm not sure I believe in all of that stuff,
though I sure would like to make my Mum eternally happy.
(To the audience) What do you think everybody? Do you think
I should touch the magic spinning wheel? **(Nooo!)** I can't
hear you. **(Nooo!)** My friends said no.

CARABOSSE
They said yes.

LUNA
They said no.

CARABOSSE
They said yes. *(To the audience)* Did you say no? **(Yes!)** See,
they said yes.

LUNA
I'm not sure that's what -

CARABOSSE
(With a fierce intensity) Listen to me carefully, young lady,
your family have thrown you out, you have no money, you
have no home. Touch the needle and your life could change
forever, don't touch the needle and it stays as miserable as it
is. Rewrite your story and make someone very close to you
very, very happy. Are you selfless or are you selfish? A loving
person or a little princess? You know what you want, so do it
before it's too late in 3, 2, 1.

> *LUNA touches the needle. There is a big flash as the cart
> wheels off on its own, CARABOSSE whips her cape off
> and LUNA is left lying on the floor in a pool of light as if
> she's under a spell. She is still alive but sapped of all
> energy.*

CARABOSSE
Surprise surprise.

LUNA
Queen Carabosse! It's you!

CARABOSSE
(In DRESSMAKER voice) Yes dear, didn't you recognise me?

LUNA
Polo! Maris! Spud! Help!

CARBOSSE
(Imitating her) 'Polo! Maris! Spud! Help!'. I'm afraid, young
lady, your little gang can't help you now.

LUNA
What have you done to me?

CARABOSSE
Feeling a little sleepy? Well in two minute's time, you'll feel
more than a little sleepy and in five minutes, you'll feel
sooooo sleepy, you'll be DEAD!

CARABOSSE cackles off, singing.

Thunder and lightening everywhere. Luna's collapses
to her knees. Uh. Oh.

MARIS, SPUD and POLO enter. Ominous underscore.

POLO
Lloh llo! (Oh no!)

MARIS
Luna! What happened? We heard you shouting.

LUNA
It's Queen Carabosse, she was in disguise and put a deadly
curse on me.

MARIS
I thought I saw someone acting suspicious.

SPUD
Yeah there's been a lot of suspicious acting tonight.

LUNA
I'm so sorry I should have listened to you all along.

MARIS
Don't be sorry, I should have come with you.

POLO
Whall llan lee lloo Luna?

LUNA
I think it's too late. I just wanted to see you to say I'm sorry.
I'm so... tired.

MARIS/SPUD/POLO
Luna, no!

> *LUNA collapses in their arms. Flash. Musical glisten.
> FAIRY-FIZZ enters.*

FAIRY-FIZZ
F to the I to the Zed Zed why? She's Fizzy!
(Whoop! Whoop!)
She's Fizzy! Oh yeah.
What's happened Maris?

MARIS
Oh Fizz. I foolishly threw Luna out of the house and wicked
Carabosse has put a deadly curse on her.

SPUD
Please help us!

FAIRY-FIZZ
A death curse, I'm afraid, is irreversible...

MARIS / SPUD / POLO
No!

FAIRY-FIZZ
...but we may be able to alter its course. With everyone's help
I can change it to a *sleeping* curse. If it works, Luna will not
die, but she will remain asleep until she is woken with true
love's kiss.

MARIS
True love's kiss?!

SPUD
Who would that be?

FAIRY-FIZZ
I have my suspicions *(With an urgency)* But first, the spell.
"Izzy Fizzy let's get busy." Everyone, say the magic words
with me. "Izzy Fizzy let's get busy."

> *A magical musical shimmer and LUNA falls asleep.*
> *Snoring.*

MARIS
You did it Fizz!

FAIRY-FIZZ
We're not out of the danger zone yet, Maris. We need to make
sure Carabosse can't get anywhere near Luna. We're going to
create an ice palace to protect her. And to do that we need to
create an ice storm. I'm going to need a helping hand. Sprites
of the Ice, I summon you.

> The ICE SPRITES appear.

SONG: WAKE ME UP / I GO TO SLEEP / I WILL GET WHAT I WANT
(FAIRY-FIZZ, ICE SPRITES, MARIS & SPUD, CARABOSSE)

SONG PART A

FAIRY FIZZ
(*To audience*) Will you help me too Fizzy Friends? **(Yes!)**
Fizz-tastic! Imagination stations at the ready, everyone. We
need to do this in stages, so when I give you the signal, kids,
I want you to rub your hands together just like this. Have a
quick practice **(They rub)**. That's great! Pause for now and
wait for my signal. Next, when Maris says 'women' I want all
you wonder women in the audience to click your fingers like
this as fast as you can like this. (*She demonstrates*) Now you
try! **(They click)**. That's it, you're naturals!

SPUD
Dads, Grandads, Uncles - All the men will be next so when I
shout 'Men' we want you to pat your thighs like this. **(They
pat)**.

MARIS
The last job needs someone very special - so [Graham] stand
up ..

    [GRAHAM] stands up.

[Graham] when I say your name I want you to wave my
special hanky frantically to get the wind going. Get it? Got it?
Good!

    Underscore cuts out. Silence.

FAIRY-FIZZ

Okay everyone we haven't much time, so close your eyes, keep them closed and *(calming everyone down)* imagine winter is on its way. *(Whispering)* Okay, start us off, kids.

The kids start rubbing their hands.

MARIS.
All the women.

The women start clicking.

SPUD.
All the men.

The men pat their knees. The overall effect is the sound of rain. SFX rumble of thunder.

FAIRY-FIZZ
That's the rainstorm starting, now wave your hanky [Graham]! Faster [Graham] Faster!

Music in. Snow falls, dry ice, the lights change to cold blues and whites.

The front cloth flies out revealing …

Scene 6 - The Ice Palace

*The stage has transformed into an ice palace with a
bier made of ice at its centre.*

SONG PART B

MARIS picks up LUNA and carries her to the bed.

FAIRY FIZZ
Maris, Spud, go get ready for your quest to find Luna's One
True Love.

They go.

And I will find out *who* it is.

When all seems hard and cold as ice
Dream of warmth and all things nice
Let your love appear to you
So I may know a heart that's true

PRINCE ISTUNA appears as if part of Luna's dream.

It's as I thought. Her true love is Prince Istuna!

*As he does LUNA's spirit leaves her body and is
momentarily reunited with him.*

SONG PART C

*We see CARABOSSE celebrating in the distance.
She Sings I Will Get What I Want! Reprise*

*LUNA's spirt returns to her sleeping body.
FIZZ and the ICE SPRITES surround her in a protective
circle.*

SONG PART D

One final flurry of snow in the auditorium.

End of Act One

ACT TWO

Scene 1 - The Ice Palace

FAIRY FIZZ and the ICE SPRITES are revealed guarding the sleeping LUNA.

Music in.

FAIRY-FIZZ
F to the I to the Zed Zed why? She's Fizzy!
(**Whoop! Whoop!)**
She's Fizzy! Oh yeah.

Thanks Fizzy Pals. With your help last night, Luna is still alive. It's now only one day until Luna's eighteenth Birthday, so the race is on to find Prince Istuna and defeat Carabozza!

SONG: I Will Be Heard!
(FAIRY-FIZZ and ICE SPRITES)

>   *After song -*
>   MARIS, SPUD and POLO enter.

MARIS
Fairy Fizz, it's brilliant what you've done with all this ice palace - very Scandi-chic retreat n'all that, but isn't this all a bit futile - Luna *has* no true love that we know of.

SPUD
She had a Harry Styles calendar one year, but his agent said he wouldn't agree to do panto.

FAIRY-FIZZ
Fear not, it's all very clear to me. Prince Istuna is our only hope.

SPUD
(to Maris) Prince's Tuna?

MARIS
(to Spud) Prince's Tuna?!

POLO
Pllinclle Istunall!

FAIRY-FIZZ
You haven't much time, you must find Prince Istuna as fast as
you can.

SPUD
Come on then, let's go!

MARIS
(Exiting) Thank you Fairy-Fizz!

> *MARIS, SPUD and POLO exit.*
> *FIZZ and ICE SPRITES resume song to end scene.*

Scene 2 - The Arctic Tundra

PRINCE ITSUNA bounds in.

PRINCE
Oh Luna! Luna! Luna! My heart will always be yours, Sweet
Luna, we only met yesterday but our love is like the wind. I
can't see it, but I can feel it all around me.

SONG: I'm So in Love!

>*The PRINCE sings alone. He is enraptured. It's his big
>number.*
>
>*After a verse, MARIS and SPUD enter in over-the-top
>winter gear complete with back-packs and binoculars.
>They have a large sign which says 'Looking for —>'
>with a picture of a tin of Prince's Tuna on it.*
>
>*They head to the PRINCE pointing at the sign, saying
>things like 'Excuse me, do you by any chance have any
>tuna?' but they are interrupting his big moment.*
>
>*The PRINCE moves away to continue singing, they
>think this is rude and follow him. He tries everything to
>get rid of them without it undermining his moment.*
>
>*MARIS searches him as if he was at airport security,
>including in his hair and his trousers. Metal detector on
>his trousers etc. SPUD stands stock still in aviators like
>an enforcer type.*
>
>*They head into the audience and cause havoc. They
>find [Graham] and search him, during which suspect
>objects reveal themselves: a fluorescent mankini, a
>framed picture of MARIS, huge pair of frilly knickers
>etc. They exit.*

PRINCE
Hello penguin, how are you? Is Luna with you?

POLO
Polo shakes his head. He mimes; 1) Carabosse was dressed as an old lady; 2) Luna pricked her finger; 3) She now lies sleeping; and 4) you must come quickly.

PRINCE
(simultaneously) No... Luna's not here because she's gone to see her Gran... who has burnt her finger... but her Gran is now having a nap... do I want to come for a jog?

POLO
Polo shakes his head, and mimes; 1) That wicked witch Carabosse cast a spell; 2) Luna died; 3) But she loves you; so 4) you need to come and kiss her.

PRINCE
(simultaneously) No that's not right... OK Harry Potter turned up... whilst you were sunbathing... then you got heartburn... and I kissed Harry Potter?

POLO is exasperated. He voices that the PRINCE is stupid.

PRINCE
No? I'm sorry. OK do it again, I'll get it this time I promise.

POLO mimes this super fast, but remarkably clearly.

POLO
1) Carabosse came on; 2) In disguise; 3) as a dressmaker; 4) with a spinning wheel; 5) Meanwhile Luna; 6) Who you love; 7) Touched the spinning wheel 8) And fell to the ground; 9) and in five minutes; 10) was dead; 11) Then Fairy Fizz

arrived; 12) to make an ice palace; 13) the audience created rain; 14) [Graham] waved his hanky; 15) I waddled here to get you -

PRINCE
(simultaneously) Carabosse was here... in disguise... as a dressmaker... with a spinning wheel... Meanwhile Luna... who I love... touched the spinning wheel... fell to the ground... and in five minutes... was dead!... Then Fairy Fizz arrived... to make an ice palace... the audience created rain... [Graham] waved his hanky... you rushed here to get me - *(suddenly able to fill in the gaps)* - because I need to hurry home with you and wake Luna with true love's kiss?

> *Music: Tada! POLO is knackered.*

Well why didn't you say so in the first place? Come on then we better get going.

> *Seductive music. Suddenly a LADY PENGUIN enters and drapes herself across the pros. POLO is instantly entranced and the PRINCE can't get his attention for love nor money.*

Polo, we really need to get a move on. Polo! Polo?

> *LADY PENGUIN claps, the lights change, and a famous love pop song plays.*

> *The PRINCE dashes off.*

SONG: PENGUIN SEDUCTION MEDLEY

> *The two love birds dance seductively towards one another. They are joined by a kick line of dancing penguins in flippers.*

*LADY PENGUIN sings, before POLO joins in with
aplomb.*

*Finally POLO and the LADY PENGUIN come towards
each other for a kiss. But at the last second, the LADY
PENGUIN grabs him in a headlock. She whips her
head off - it is CARABOSSE! Dun Dun Dunnnn!*

CARABOSSE
Gotcha. Fell for that one didn't you. I'm rather enjoying this
dressing up game.

POLO
Clallaboss!

CARABOSSE
Hello Polo, fancy coming back to mine for a light supper? I'm
having Aromatic Crispy Penguin. *(To a shaking Polo)* And they
say frightened meat tastes better.

*She boinks POLO over the head with her sceptre. He
collapses, out cold.*

CARABOSSE
Oh dear, dear, dear, what will they all do now? I know that
Foolish Fizz Pop Fairy is up to something so I'm taking extra
measures. I'm going to eat Luna's pet Penguin for my din
dins. And if she has survived, she's bound to come running to
the castle where I can put an end to her once and for all!
(Boo!) Nobody can stop me, and if any of you even try, I'll
release a box of toe nibbling rats into the auditorium. **(Boo!)**
Oh how many times do I have to flush to get rid of you lot?

*CARABOSSE exits, dragging POLO and laughing
maniacally.*

Scene 3 - The Ice Palace

LUNA is asleep on the ice bier. SPUD and MARIS are eating sandwiches out of tin foil.

SPUD looks at the sky. Gentle underscore.

SPUD
Look Mum. Red sky at night, shepherd's delight. Blue sky at night, day.

MARIS
Spud, it's no use. Only one day from her eighteenth Birthday and look at the poor thing. I don't think we'll ever wake poor Luna.

SPUD
We must try and keep our hopes up, mum.

MARIS
[Graham], as I'm feeling low, will you kiss me under the mistletoe?... What d'ya mean you wouldn't kiss me under anaesthetic?!

SFX: Knock-knock at the door.

SPUD
Who's there?

PRINCE
Mrs Piper?

SPUD
It's the Tesco delivery, mum. I'll let him in.

Disappears but reappears almost immediately with the PRINCE.

Come in, come in, just leave the bags by the body, anything for the freezer I'll take from you separately.

PRINCE
Maris Piper?

SPUD
Potatoes? They go straight in the cupboard.

PRINCE
(Seeing the sleeping princess) Poor Luna, how could Carabosse do this to her?! *(To Spud and Maris)* Apologies, I am Prince Istuna. Your penguin told me of her plight and I've come to reverse the curse.

SPUD
You're Prince Istuna? And here to reverse the curse? And Polo the Piper penguin reported poor Luna's plight to you?

PRINCE
Polo the Piper penguin reported poor Luna's plight at a pace, so I could reverse the curse at a pace pacier than the space race.

SPUD
(By now in rhythm and at speed)
So you purport from Polo's report (that's Polo the Piper penguin)
Poor Luna is placed n' her face's embraced at a pace exceeding the space race
And you propose to that 'purpoze' the person reversin' the curse then,
Should be you today, mum whaddya say?? -

MARIS
I say Spud you're an idiot.

PRINCE
Mrs Piper, may I kiss your hand?

MARIS
Why is my face dirty?

PRINCE
Please listen to me, to save Luna I must kiss her.

MARIS
Are you suggesting I should let you kiss this helpless young
lady whilst she's lying here asleep unable to say no?

PRINCE
Well I wouldn't put it like that ..

  She slaps him (SFX cartoon loud slap).

MARIS
And are you suggesting I should let her be smooched by a
stranger in tights on the pretence she 'might live to breathe
another day'?

PRINCE
Well I wouldn't put it like that ..

  She slaps him again (SFX cartoon loud slap).

MARIS
And are you suggesting I should let her be canoodled by a
sexy young man with the same name as a supermarket fish
product?

PRINCE
Well that's where the mix up is ..

  She slaps him again (SFX cartoon loud slap).

SPUD
Mum wait! I don't think you understand. This isn't Prince's
Tuna, this is Prince Istuna.

*She punches Spud and floors him (SFX cartoon loud
punch).*

Bang. FAIRY-FIZZ appears.

FAIRY-FIZZ
F to the I to the Zed Zed why? She's Fizzy!
(Whoop! Whoop!)
She's Fizzy! Oh yeah.

MARIS
Oh Fizz, you're just in time. This gorgeous young scallywag is
trying to snog our Luna while she's kipping.

FAIRY-FIZZ
And you mustn't stand in his way!

MARIS
(To PRINCE) You see I told you! *(To FIZZ)* Yer what?

PRINCE
Mrs Piper, I am a Prince, and my name is Istuna. I met Luna
yesterday and fell madly in love with her.

FAIRY-FIZZ
And she with him. The Prince is Luna's one true love. She told
me in a dream.

SPUD
Quick, Princey, before it's too late.

SONG: I Want to Make You Better.

Intro. The PRINCE prepares himself.

PRINCE
What if it doesn't work?

FIZZ
You'll never know if you don't give it try.

The PRINCE kneels by LUNA.

MARIS
(to Spud) Ooh how exciting, it's like an episode of Love Island
this.

The PRINCE sings, then kisses her on the forehead.
With a sudden swell of music. LUNA is revived.

LUNA
Maris, Spud!

MARIS and SPUD
Luna!!

PRINCE
It worked!

LUNA
Prince Istuna, you… you brought me back to life.

PRINCE
With the help of Fairy Fizz of course.

LUNA
All of you, thank you so much.

PRINCE
It was really Polo who saved you. He sent me here to find
you.

SPUD
That was brilliant. True love's kiss, happy ever after. *(Exiting with Maris) We'll* be in the bar by nine fifteen.

LUNA
Wait a minute!

They all stop.

Where's Polo now?

FAIRY-FIZZ
I'm afraid Polo has been captured by Carabosse and taken back to the castle.

LUNA
Oh no!

MARIS
That's awful!

SPUD
That's terrible! Be more like nine *thirty* now.

LUNA
We must go and rescue him straight away.

FAIRY FIZZ
Wait a minute Luna. This will be a trap.

LUNA
A trap?

FAIRY FIZZ
To lure you to the castle.

LUNA

Why me? How have I upset her so much? I only invited her to my birthday.

FAIRY FIZZ
Maris? Spud? I think it's time.

MARIS and SPUD nod. Underscore.

Luna. Carabosse isn't the real Queen. She is only Queen Regent until the royal princess is old enough to take the throne. She will do *anything* to prevent that happening.

LUNA
I don't understand.

FAIRY-FIZZ
When the King and Queen mysteriously disappeared, I witnessed Carabosse abandoning the baby princess in the woods. Once she had gone I took the child to an ordinary village lady and her son.

MARIS
(under her breath) Who's she calling 'ordinary'?

FAIRY-FIZZ
I asked her to look after the princess and protect her and keep her hidden away from Carabosse until she was old enough to be queen herself... Tomorrow, that Royal baby / will turn eighteen.

LUNA
/ will turn eighteen.

Beat

MARIS
Oh Luna, I'm sorry. I've wanted to tell you so many times.

SPUD
Me too. Every time you went to the toilet I wanted to say
that's a Royal Flush. Every time you did a number one I
wanted to say it's the Royal Wee. And every time you made a
big mistake in life I wanted to say well you've ROYALLY -

MARIS / PRINCE / FIZZ
Spud!

SPUD
-CKED THAT UP!

LUNA
Then you're not my real Mum.

MARIS
No, love.

LUNA
And Queen Carabosse...

FAIRY FIZZ
Is your Aunt.

LUNA
But that means my real Mum and Dad... were the King and
Queen.

FAIRY-FIZZ
They didn't abandon you, Luna. They loved you very much
and they'd do anything to make you happy.

LUNA
Like touching a magic spinning wheel.

PRINCE
What do you mean?

LUNA
I think Carabosse must've placed the same curse on my
mother and father.

PRINCE
Your Aunt sounds like quite a piece of work.

SPUD
(to PRINCE) Mate - a lot of family drama for someone you
met yesterday. I'd get out now if I were you.

LUNA
I must go to the castle and save Polo.

PRINCE
I'm coming with you.

FAIRY-FIZZ
Be careful, Luna. Carabosse is pure evil.

LUNA
All the more reason she must be stopped.

SPUD
Well then we're coming too. Right Mum? Polo would do
anything for us so we'll do anything to save him, right?

MARIS
Right!

PRINCE
We should split up and approach the castle from opposite
directions, right?

ALL
Right!

PRINCE

You three go left and we'll go right.

ALL
Right.

SPUD
Which way do we go?

ALL
Left.

SPUD
(*agreeing*) Right.

ALL
(*correcting*) Left!

SPUD
(*agreeing*) Right!

ALL
(*correcting*) Left!

SPUD
(*army major-like*) Right, left!

LUNA
Listen Spud, I need you to concentrate. We need to be strong!

SPUD
(*punching*) Phmmp!

LUNA
Brave!

SPUD
(*arm shields*) Huzzah!

LUNA
And cunning!

SPUD
(*mysterious and wizard like*) I'm a little teapot.

SONG: I Will Be Heard! *Reprise*
(PRINCE, LUNA, MARIS, SPUD, FIZZ, TOWNSFOLK)

> *After Song -*
>
> *MARIS, SPUD and FIZZ head one way, Prince and Luna go the other.*

Scene 4 - Haunted Corridor

CARABOSSE appears.

CARABOSSE
Do you like my art gallery? I didn't really like the originals so
I used an AI platform to improve them a little. Far cheaper
than dealing with the artists and fewer egos involved. After
all, artists are just children who refused to put down their
crayons.

SFX: Beep Beep Beep. She holds up a biscuit.

VOICEOVER
'Alert - the enemy is in the castle'.

CARABOSSE
Aha, this artificially intelligent Jammy Dodger has just told me
that Luna and her ludicrous lemmings have taken the bait and
are approaching the castle... This is one smart cookie.

Music in

Cookie. Prepare for 'Operation Fear'!

SFX: Beep Beep Beep

VOICEOVER
Instruction received.

CARABOSSE
Luna...

SONG: You Won't Get Past Me!
(CARABOSSE)

After a verse, her DEMONS start to creep in.

Then, at the end of the song -

SFX: Beep Beep Beep

VOICEOVER
Alert. Operation Fear - Ready for Execution.

CARABOSSE
Excellent. I think the castle corridor might be a little haunted by the time those idiots arrive. Gives me a time to be 'ready for execution' of another kind.

CARABOSSE exits as MARIS, SPUD and FIZZ enter.

FIZZ
Come on you two, I think we're nearly there.

MARIS
Ooh it's such a long way. I'm absolutely knickered.

SPUD
Do you mean knackered?

MARIS
No, knickered. My breath's coming in short pants - listen, here.

She pushes his ear to her chest.

Can you hear my heart pounding?

SFX Thunder and lightning.

SPUD
I can hear your stomach rumbling. Oh I don't like it here, look at all these shifty faces. It's like a cabinet meeting at Number Ten.

MARIS
I don't think it's all that bad. Reminds me of when Michelangelo said he wanted to do me up on the ceiling.

    SFX spooky noise.

SPUD
What's that, mum?

FAIRY-FIZZ
That, is the unmistakable sound of a man eating demon.

    SFX More spooky noises. Spud starts physically panicking.

SPUD
Aaahh!

MARIS
Calm down, Spud, the only thing to fear is fear itself...

SPUD
Fear itself.

MARIS
...And demons!!

SPUD
AAAAAGHHHHH

MARIS
WILL YOU STOP IT SPUD!

FAIRY FIZZ
I know, why don't we sing a song to keep our spirits up?

SPUD
Good idea. What are we going to sing?

MARIS
Well, I know how to sing 'You Sexy Thing'

SPUD
And I know how to dance, you ugly mug.

FAIRY FIZZ
I can sing 'Under the Sea'.

SPUD
I can sing in the shower.

MARIS
I can sing 'Like a Virgin'.

SPUD
I wish you'd behave like one.

FAIRY FIZZ
I know, why don't we sing 'La Bamba[3]'?

SPUD
That's a brilliant idea and we can pretend we're British tourists on holiday in sunny Mexico to distract ourselves.

MARIS
Very good. Are you sitting comfortably?

----

[3] A licence issued to perform this play does not include permission to use the music specified in this copy.

SPUD/FAIRY-FIZZ
Err -

MARIS
- Good. Then we'll begin.

SPUD
Hit it, Uncle Paul!

> *Music. The band play but the music is decidedly limp
> and slow, soon to be stopped by Maris and Spud.*

Hang on a minute, hang on Uncle Paul. What are you doing,
we don't want it like that.

SPUD
No we need it much more upbeat, like erm *(big singing and
AIR-MARACAS-ING)* DINKA DINKA DINKA DA DINK -

SPUD and FAIRY FIZZ
     (continuing together)
- Do do do doo d d dinka dinka dinka da dink

MARIS
Yes that's much better. Can you and the band do that for us
Uncle Paul? Excellent, okay, I'll count you in: one, two, three,
four!

BAND
     (An accurate impression)
DINKA DINKA DINKA DA DINK Do do do doo d d dinka dinka
dinka da dink.

MARIS
     (to the audience)
Don't encourage them everyone, they don't get out much.
Right, do it properly this time. Okay here we go:

SONG: La Bamba w/intro 1
   (MARIS, FIZZ and SPUD)

> *As Fizz sings, Maris and Spud dance out of the left hand door.*
>
> *MARIS and SPUD return through the right hand door. MARIS holding a cocktail and SPUD with an inflatable flamingo.*

SPUD
It's a lovely song, but I still feel frightened.

FAIRY-FIZZ
I've got an idea, Spud: Fizzy friends out front, if you see anything untoward, will you shout as loudly as you can and tell us? **(Yes)** Will you? **(Yes!)**

MARIS
Brilliant! Right we'll come straight in this time - on the ball, Uncle Paul: one two seven six three.

SONG: La Bamba w/o intro 2

> *MARIS and SPUD head off through the doors again but as they do a DEMON comes on and dances behind FIZZ.*
>
> *The DEMON exits as SPUD and MARIS return with more holiday props.*

MARIS, FIZZ and SPUD
Did something untoward happen? **(Yes)** What was it? **(A Demon)** Where was it? **(Behind you)** Behind us?! **(Yes)**

FIZZ

We'll sing it again then but this time you have to shout much, much louder. On the ball, Uncle Paul: one two five seven three.

SONG: La Bamba w/o intro 3

> *MARIS and SPUD head off through the door. As FIZZ sings three DEMONS dance around her.*
>
> *As the DEMONS exit, MARIS returns with a cactus, and SPUD returns in an inflatable donkey costume.*

MARIS, FIZZ and SPUD
Did something untoward happen? **(Yes)** What was it? **(A demon)** Where was it? **(Behind you)** Behind us?! **(Yes)**

SPUD
Alright we'll sing it again then and this time shout much, much louder. On the ball, Uncle Paul: one nine nine nine three.

SONG: La Bamba w/o intro 4

> *MARIS and SPUD head off through the door. As FIZZ sings more demons dance around her and carry her off.*
>
> *MARIS and SPUD return with more inflatables and holiday props.*

SPUD
Hey Mum. Looks like someone's run off with Fairy Fizz!

MARIS / SPUD
Did something untoward happen? **(Yes)** What was it? **(A demon)** Where was it? **(Behind you)** Behind us?! **(Yes)**

MARIS
Alright Spud you sing it this time and you lot shout much, much, much louder. On the ball, Uncle Paul: One two Three-ee-ee.

SONG: La Bamba w/o intro 5

> *MARIS head off through the door. As SPUD sings the DEMONS dance around him and carry him off.*
>
> *MARIS comes back with more inflatables and holiday props.*

MARIS
It looks like someone's just made off with Spud. (*Frightened*) Was it a demon? **(Yes!)** Why didn't you tell me? **(We did!)** Okay - well to pass the time we'll sing it very quietly this time. This time after two: one one one one TWO.

SONG: La Bamba 6

> *As she sings DEMONS invade the auditorium and the stage. Eventually all the DEMONS end up on the stage and start dancing with MARIS in a salsa line holding maracas.*
>
> *The music stops but MARIS continues riffing wildly.*
>
> *Eventually she stops, she looks to her right and then to her left as the DEMONS stare at her. She looks out and goes to scream, but the demons scream first and run off.*

MARIS
Charming! (*Exiting*) Is it because of my prickly cactus?

> *Cloth out.*

Scene 5 - Carabosse's Evil Lair

CARABOSSE is revealed centre stage. POLO is in the cage. The DEMONS surround him.

CARABOSSE
Now then, what's black and white and goes round and round? A Penguin in a microwave. *(Polo responds)* No don't worry Polo, I won't put you in the microwave, I'll put you in the mincer instead. I better wash my hands before we prepare dinner. Go and lay the table, demons.

They exit.

LUNA and PRINCE climb in through the window, Mission Impossible style.

PRINCE
The coast is clear, come on.

They rush to POLO. He is panicking.

LUNA
Polo! There you are. I'm so glad you're still alive. Where is the key?

POLO
Llalabosse! Llalabosse!

LUNA
Carabosse has it!? Ok you don't need to worry, Polo. I have a foolproof plan. We'll have you out of here in no time. Istuna, over here.

PRINCE and LUNA duck down on the other side.

PRINCE
Does this sort of stuff happen to you every day?

LUNA
Yesterday I was looking for party hats. Today I'm a Princess in a castle trying to defeat my wicked dictator Aunt whilst my-my real-parents-who-no-longer-exist were actually the real King and Queen and my family-who-are-not-my-family have been *lying* to me. I guess royalty looks easier from the outside.

PRINCE
I don't know. There are many things you don't have to worry about when you're royal. Like paying the rent on your house.

LUNA
Oh yeah. Another thing I no longer have.

PRINCE
You don't have a foolproof plan either do you?

LUNA
No. But Polo doesn't need to know that. I don't want him to worry. I've looked after him since he was born and I'll do anything to protect him from danger.

PRINCE
Even if it means lying to him?

LUNA
Huh?... Oh.

SONG: I Really Like This Person! (Reprise)

> They kiss. POLO coughs. *'What about me?'*
> SPUD, MARIS and FIZZ enter.

SPUD
(*Loudly*) Alright kids! (*Alright Spud*)

LUNA, PRINCE and POLO
Ssshhh!

SPUD
(*quietly*) Alright kids! *(Alright Spud)*

MARIS
(*quietly*)
Hi-de-hi folks (**Ho-de-ho Maris**). Hi-de-hi Graham (**Ho-de-ho Maris**).

FAIRY-FIZZ
(*quietly*) F to the I to the Zed Zed why? She's Fizzy!
(Whoop! Whoop!)
She's Fizzy! Oh yeah.

LUNA
Okay you three, we need to get the key off Carabosse in order to release Polo. Spud, I need you to concentrate. You must be smart!

SPUD
Two twos are four!

LUNA
Fast!

SPUD
(*Quickly*) Two twos are four!

LUNA
And unpredictable!

SPUD
Two-twos are for ballet.

CARABOSSE wanders on next to SPUD, who doesn't notice her. The others look on aghast.

Listen guys, you don't have to worry about me, I've got it all sorted, because if anyone finds me and says...

CARABOSSE
Hello.

SPUD
I'll just be like 'Hello to you too'. And if they're like -

CARABOSSE
What exactly do you think you're doing?

SPUD
I'll be like, 'I'm just hanging out with meany Queeny Carabeany'. And then I'll be like, 'Hey what's the difference between Carabosse and a walrus?'.

CARABOSSE
I don't know, what *is* the difference between Carabosse and a walrus?

SPUD
'One has a moustache and smells of fish and the other is a walrus.'

He laughs uncontrollably. CARABOSSE taps him.

What?

CARABOSSE
Hello.

SPUD
Aggghhh!

CARABOSSE
Demons!

The DEMONS enter from all entrances enclosing them all.

I'm feeling hungry. Prepare the mincer!

MARIS
Hey, who are you calling a mincer?!

CARABOSSE
Oh shut up.

SPUD
Oi! You can't talk to my Mum like that, you're not half the man she is.

PRINCE
Carabosse. Where is the key to Polo's cage?

CARABOSSE
Around my neck, if you want it you'll have to fight me for it.

PRINCE
All right then I will.

CARABOSSE
Demons! Arrest the Prince!

They restrain him.

LUNA
In that case *I'll* fight you for it.

Everyone stops and looks at LUNA.

MARIS
Luna, don't be so silly.

LUNA
What do you say, Aunt Carabosse, shall we settle this score
once and for all? I'll take you on myself.

CARABOSSE
Oh goodie. She's pretending to be grown up again. In that
case I'll play dress-up too.

> *She clicks her fingers and the lights go out.*

Cookie. Prepare for 'Operation Fire'!

> *SFX: Beep Beep Beep*

VOICEOVER
Operation Fire Executed.

> *Lights up. Music. Carabosse has been replaced with a
> fire breathing dragon.*

UNDERSCORE: THE FIGHT

> *LUNA battles with the DRAGON as MARIS, FIZZ, SPUD
> and the PRINCE take on the DEMONS.*

> *LUNA manages to snatch the key from the DRAGON'S
> neck. She passes it to the the PRINCE but a DEMON
> snatches it from him. But FIZZ snatches it off the
> DEMON. But a DEMON snatches it off of FIZZ. But
> MARIS snatches it off of the DEMON and passes it to
> SPUD who drops it but retrieves it and opens the cage
> and frees POLO. The DRAGON has cornered LUNA and
> is about to eat her when the POLO pulls on its tail. The
> DRAGON roars with rage.*

POLO
LLun llevelleron llun! (Run everyone run)

LUNA
Come on everyone - let's get out of here.

> *Our heroes scarper. POLO releases the DRAGON and
> waddles after them.*

CARABOSSE
After them you fools!

> *The DRAGON and DEMONS set off in hot pursuit.*

Scene 6 - The Arctic Tundra/Forest

As we hear the voice of CARABOSSE singing we see our heroes being pursued by the DRAGON and DEMONIC HORDE in various different formations. Throughout the sequence our heroes run across the tundra and through the forest.

Song: You Won't Get Past Me! Reprise
(CARABOSSE)

After a chorus, the music suddenly switches to an Irish instrumental theme and the entire company - baddies and goodies - dance Irish dance. You Won't Get Passed Me! resumes and the DRAGON runs on and chases everyone off.

CARABOSSE resumes singing - then - Instrumental underscore. MARIS and SPUD run on.

MARIS.
We need to stop this dragon, will you help us? **(Yes!)** Brilliant! Now I've put a potato under every seat in the theatre. I want you to reach down and grab it. Then hold it in the air and shout 'potato!' **(Potato!)** That's it hold them taties up high so we can see them.

SPUD
Now when we we shout "One, Two, Three Monster Mash" we want to you throw your potatoes at the dragon. Hopefully knocking it out and letting us escape.

MARIS
Can everyone remember the signal? **(Yes)** We shout "One, Two, Three Monster Mash" and you throw the potatoes, mashing that monster. Ready? **(Yes!)** Now spuds at the ready, keep your eyes peeled and get ready to mash.

More chasing backwards and forwards.

You Won't Get Past Me! Reprise - then -
The DRAGON appears.

MARIS and SPUD.
ONE, TWO THREE, MONSTER MASH!

The audience pelt the DRAGON with potatoes! It runs
off with its tail between its legs.
Scared dog - SFX

MARIS
We did it!

FAIRY-FIZZ
Three cheers for Maris's Potatoes for saving the day. Hip hip!
(Hooray). Hip hip! **(Hooray).** Hip hip! **(Hooray).**

The cloth flies out revealing ...

Scene 7 - The Town Square

SPUD
Nice one, Mum, you're going to go down in history here in
Colchester, with great legends like Boudica and Dermot
O'Leary!

Flash. CARABOSSE enters.

CARABOSSE
Thought you could get away from me did you? Haven't you
forgotten about my magic powers?

Watch out Luna, say goodbye.
With this spell you're sure to die.

She casts the spell, a pyro fires nearby.

LUNA
Ha! You missed.

PRINCE
(Jumping in front of Luna) Carabosse, if you're after Luna
you'll have to kill me first.

LUNA
No, Istuna, no!

CARABOSSE
Fine then Princey, say farewell,
Now you'll *both* die with this spell.

She casts the spell, a pyro fires nearby.

LUNA
Ha! You missed again.

SPUD
(putting himself in the line of fire) Candyfloss, if you're after
Luna and Princey you'll have to kill *me* first.

LUNA and PRINCE
No, Spud, no!

SPUD
Come on Queeny, do your best,
Get it off your hairy chest.

> *She casts the spell. SPUD is struck with almighty pain
> running through him and falls slowly to the ground. The
> stage goes red as lightening flashes and music suggests
> the end is nigh.*

SPUD
You got me! Aaagh, help, I can't breath, the pain *etc.*

ALL
Spud! No! Help! Someone do something! Please no! *etc.*

> *Music out. Huge fart SFX. Lights revert.*

SPUD
Sorry, I had some baked beans earlier. You definitely missed
me though.

> *Commotion re: SPUD and his beans.*

CARABOSSE
Silence! Fools! I'll not take defeat.
Your houses are mine, so get out on the street!

> *Flash. FAIRY-FIZZ appears.*

FAIRY-FIZZ
F to the I to the Zed Zed why? She's Fizzy!

(Whoop! Whoop!)
She's Fizzy! Oh yeah.

(Rapping)
Hold it right there, Fizzy me's had enough
This story needs an ending, its time to get tough!
Listen, Colchester, I've news for you all
She doesn't own your houses at all

MARIS
Yes she does, Fairy-Fizz. As Queen she owns and controls the Kingdom.

FAIRY-FIZZ
She's only the queen if the child is too young
That's why she's been, recently, so highly strung
Just dreading the day when the child turned eighteen.
That's right, Princess Luna, *you* are now Queen.

>	*SFX: Clock chimes twelve with dramatic regal, sparkly music, as an ensemble member, head to toe in black, comes in and takes the royal sceptre from CARABOSSE and transfers it to LUNA. Everyone looks on in awe.*

CARABOSSE
No, please, no.

LUNA
I'm the Queen?!

FAIRY-FIZZ
Yes girl, and *because* you're the Queen, you can set the rents as low as you like.

LUNA
In that case I'll scrap them altogether.

ALL

Hooray!

LUNA
And bring back parties.

ALL
Hooray!!

SPUD
Wait what about meany-meany-now-ex-queeny?

MARIS
Yeah, what do you think everyone, what shall we do with her?
(Kill her/boil her etc.)

LUNA
What do *you* think Fairy-Fizz?

FAIRY-FIZZ
       (Casting a spell)
Mistress of deception, ex-monarch of disguise
Let us see you change your ways before our very eyes
Not to something evil though, do you really think I could?
It's time to change forever to a character that's good.

CARABOSSE
(being caught under a spell) No no no, please!

       *She's immediately replaced by the FEMALE PENGUIN
       who danced with POLO earlier.
       She does a short tap dancing flourish with POLO.*

ALL
Hooray/yay/whoop/oh wow!

SPUD
Oh wow, isn't this brilliant?! Luna's found Princey, Mum's

going home with Graham, and Polo's got his own penguin girlfriend too. *(Starting to cry)* I love it when everyone around me is in a relationship **(Aah)**.

MARIS
(Whisper) Spud you're not the only single person here, what about *(nodding towards FAIRY-FIZZ)* MmmmMmm-Mmm?

SPUD
What, me and MmmmMmm-Mmm? *(Low self esteem)* Naaahhh.

MARIS
Well if you don't ask you'll never find out.

> *Everyone mutters words of encouragement. He kneels down nervously in front of FAIRY-FIZZ.*

SPUD
Fairy-Fizz?

FAIRY-FIZZ
Yes bro?

> *He clears his throat. Crunch time.*

SPUD
Roses are red
Violets are blue
I like spaghetti
Let's get it on

MARIS
Spud!

SPUD
What?

FAIRY-FIZZ
    (rapping)
Don't worry Spud, I get it that you're keen
But let's take it slow, tho, y'know what I mean?
As it's early days, bro, I'd like to get to know ya
So why don't we hang out, yo, n' maybe give it a go yeah?

    *All cheer over 8 counts. Spud puts on a cap and
    sunglasses like FAIRY-FIZZ.
    MARIS beatboxes for him.*

SPUD
Just like spaghetti, I am your biggest fan.
I know I'm just a boy, but I'll try and be a man.
This is so cool, I give you all my thanks
I'm so happy, I've peed in my pants

ALL
Spud!

    *And suddenly the PRINCE looks like he's about to say
    something...*

Sshh.

PRINCE
Princess Luna, before I propose, is there someone I should
ask for permission first?

SPUD
Nah, just get on with it Princey.

LUNA
Yes there is actually. I'd like you to ask my mum, Maris, who's
also the best dad a girl could wish for.

    They hug.

MARIS
Oh Luna, I'm going to cry.

PRINCE
Well Dame Maris, what do you think, do I have your permission?

MARIS
Permission? I'd *love* to marry you, Princey.

SPUD
Not you, Mum! Luna!

MARIS
Oh Sorry. Sorry Luna. *(To Graham)* Sorry Graham. *(To Prince)* Sorry Princey, yes of course you can!

PRINCE
	(Down on one knee)
Queen Luna, will you marry me?

LUNA
Oh yes I will!

	Playout. Cloth in.

Scene 8 - Finale

SONG: WALK DOWN - Let's Get Married!

LUNA
Our pantomime is over
The town's no longer sad

PRINCE
Luna's found herself a Prince

SPUD
And [Graham]'s my new dad.

MARIS
My daughter has been crowned the Queen
A reward for all our toils
So I've changed my name from Maris Piper.
We're now the Jersey Royals

CARABOSSE
I've decided to be happy now
It's fun I must confess.

FAIRY-FIZZ
My fizzles you're the bizzle
Have you enjoyed yourselves? **(Yes)**

PRINCE
Merry Christmas then to all of you
Have a wonderful new year...

SPUD
If you want another song, Colchester,
Come on let's hear you cheer!

SONG: BELIEVE!

THE END

For more information on
Guy Unsworth's work, please visit:

www.guyunsworth.com

www.ingramcontent.com/pod-product-compliance
Lightning Source LLC
Chambersburg PA
CBHW050958050726
47592CB00007B/2622